I am READING

Book 2

Iam books

I am Reading **Book 2**

© 2010 I am Books

Published by
I am Books
327-32 1116ho, Daeroung Techno Town 12cha
Gasan-dong, Kumcheon-gu, Seoul, Korea 153-802
Tel 82-2-6343-0999
Fax 82-2-6343-0995~6
www.iambooks.co.kr

Publisher Sangwook Oh, Sunghyun Shin
Author Sabrina Leigh
Editor Euna Yun, Kieun Lee
Design Design Didot
Illustrated by Ilsun Lee
Marketing Shindong Jang, Shinkuk Jo, Misun Jang

ISBN 978-89-6398-036-2 64740

Preface

I am Books Reading Series is a series of reading comprehension books for beginner learners. Each student book includes 20 units, and there is an interesting and informative story in each unit. With those interesting and informative stories, students will improve their English skills simply by engaging themselves in the text.

Informative stories with lots of interesting facts about people, places, and animals will enable students to foster their creativity as well as their knowledge.

The detailed illustrations will help students understand the unit story and vocabulary.

Even though it's called a "Reading" series, it actually integrates listening, reading, writing, and speaking through **various activities and exercises**. Fun and strategic exercises and activities will provide students great opportunities to expand essential expressions and their vocabulary with high frequency words, as well as develop and improve reading fluency with strategic reading skills.

Audio CD is included so that learners can listen to the speech of native speakers and promote development of listening and pronunciation skills.

"Reading" means "Understanding" in this series.
"Understanding" means a good reader, a good speaker, and a good writer at the same time.

I believe students can become better readers and writers as they go through this series.

Do not forget,
"There is no loyal road to learning."

Sincerely

Sabrina Leigh

CONTENTS

Structures & Features

Each unit has an **interesting story** accompanied by eye-catching **illustrations**.

'Pre-read' helps students **think in advance** about the topic of a story.

Students will also improve their listening skills by listening to the **Audio CD**.

It helps students improve their **listening skills** and enrich their **vocabulary and spelling skills**.

Key sentences and words of each unit are presented to let students practice.

It helps students focus on **specific details** of the stories and improve their **reading comprehension skills**.

Self-Assessment Charts are designed to assess students understanding of the concepts, reading skills, or attitudes they are trying to learn.

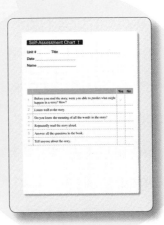

There are **various activities and exercises** for teachers, parents, and kids featuring educational games, cartoons, coloring pages, crafts, and more!

Unit 1

The Sphinx

Pre-read

- Was the sphinx real?
- Can you explain the features about the sphinx?
- Why did the ancients make the sphinx?

Track 01

The sphinx is not a real creature.

It is a creature from myths.

Its shape is very strange.

It has a human's face and a monster's body.

We can see it in Giza, Egypt, and

we guess it guarded the pyramids.

According to the myth, the sphinx waited for travelers

and gave them a riddle.

The travelers had to answer the riddle.

If they did not, the sphinx swallowed them.

Nobody could answer the riddle, except brave Oedipus.

Do you know the answer to the sphinx's riddle?

"What creature goes on four feet in the morning,

two feet at noon and three in the evening?"

8

Word Listening

Track 01

Listen and check.

1

ⓐ ⓑ ⓒ

2

ⓐ

ⓑ

Listen and write.

Oedipus	creature

3

Nobody could answer the riddle, except brave

☐☐☐☐☐☐☐ .

4

What ☐☐☐☐☐☐☐☐

goes on four feet in the morning, two feet at noon and three in the evening?

P·a·r·t 2 Picture Reading

Trace and read the story aloud.

sphinx's riddle   swallowed   myth   guarded   creature

1 The sphinx is not a real _____ .

creature

2 We can see it in Giza, Egypt, and we guess it _____ the pyramids.

guarded

3 According to the _____ , the sphinx waited for travelers and gave them a riddle.

myth

4 If they did not, the sphinx _____ them.

swallowed

5 Do you know the answer to the _____ ?

sphinx's riddle

10

Core Reading

1 This story is about _____ .

   ⓐ Egypt   ⓑ the pyramid   ⓒ the sphinx

2 According to myth, who solved the sphinx's riddle?

   ⓐ Giza
   ⓑ Nobody
   ⓒ Oedipus

 Reading Power III

Real or Make-Believe

Write Real or Make-Believe.

_____

_____

_____

_____

_____

_____

Unit 2 Beethoven Virus

Pre-read

ⓐ Who was Beethoven?

ⓑ Do you know any of his music?

ⓒ How many symphonies did he compose?

ⓓ What was his serious trouble?

Track 02

His full name is Ludwig van Beethoven.

He was born in 1770 in Bonn, Germany.

Who was he? Right! He was Beethoven, you know.

He composed symphonies and sonatas.

When he was four years old,

he played the harpsichord and violin.

He composed music and played the organ

when he was only eight.

Although he was given the grace of God, he was not happy.

When he was 30, he was almost deaf.

But, he imagined melodies in his head and wrote the music.

He died in 1827, but his music is played all over the world.

And, we still catch his musical virus.

Listening Power

Word Listening
Track 02

Listen and check.

1 ⓐ   ⓑ   ⓒ

2 ⓐ    ⓑ    ⓒ

Listen and write.

composed music	played the harpsichord

3
When he was four years old, he

□□□□□□□
□□□□□□□□□

and violin.

4

He □□□□□□□
□□□□ and played the organ
when he was only eight.

P·a·r·t 2 Picture Reading

Trace and read the story aloud.

Germany   grace   musical virus   music   sonatas

1 He was born in 1770 in Bonn, .

Germany

2 He composed symphonies and .

sonatas

3 Although he was given the of God, he was not happy.

grace

4 But, he imagined melodies in his head and wrote the .

music

5 He died in 1827, but his music is played all over the world. And, we still catch his .

musical virus

14

P·a·r·t **3** Reading Power II

Core Reading

1 This story is about _____.

   @ Antonin Dvorak   ⓑ Wolfgang Amadeus Mozart
   © Ludwig van Beethoven

2 When did Beethoven compose music and play the organ?

   @ When he was 4 years old.
   ⓑ When he was 8 years old.
   © When he was 30 years old.

P·a·r·t **4** Reading Power III

Author's Purpose

Write 'entertain,' 'inform,' or 'persuade.'

- Authors write to teach you about something.
  ➡ The author's purpose is to inform.
- Authors write to make you laugh or feel happy, sad, scared etc.
  ➡ The author's purpose is to entertain.
- Authors write to convince you to think, feel, or act a certain way.
  ➡ The author's purpose is to persuade.

1 Ludwig van Beethoven was born in 1770 in Bonn, Germany. He died in 1827, but his music is played all over the world.

   ➡ The author's purpose is to _____.

2 We still catch Beethoven's musical virus.

   ➡ The author's purpose is to _____.

3 Symphony No.9 Choral was composed by Beethoven. If you're looking for a great symphony, listen to this!

   ➡ The author's purpose is to _____.

Unit 3 Proofreading

Pre-read

a What is the meaning of proof?

b What is proofreading?

c Why do we need proofreading?

Track 03

What is proofreading?

It means to look over and check carefully.

Writers look over sentences and check spelling.

They also don't forget to check grammar,

punctuation, and other errors.

They proofread every detail.

Why do they do it carefully?

The answer is simple.

For the readers!

Then, only writers proofread? No.

You need to proofread what you write.

Before submitting your report or homework, proofread it!

Word Listening

Track 03

Listen and check.

1 ⓐ   ⓑ error
   ~~errer~~   ⓒ ___V___

2 ⓐ    ⓑ

Listen and write.

errors	proofreading

3    What is ☐☐☐☐☐
   -☐☐☐☐☐☐☐ ?

4    They also don't forget to check grammar,
   punctuation, and other
   ☐☐☐☐☐☐ .

P·a·r·t 2 Picture Reading

Trace and read the story aloud.

proofread   readers   punctuation   write   writers

1 They also don't forget to check grammar, . , ! " " ' ', and other errors.

punctuation

2 The answer is simple. For the !

readers

3 Then, only proofread? No.

writers

4 You need to proofread what you .

write

5 Before submitting your report or homework, it!

proofread

Reading Power II

Part 3 Core Reading

1 This story is about _____.

    ⓐ checking for spelling   ⓑ proofreading marks
    ⓒ proofreading

2 Which of the following about the reading is NOT true?

    ⓐ Writers check for grammar, punctuation, and other errors.
    ⓑ Only writers proofread.
    ⓒ Students proofread their own reports.

Writing Power

Part 4 Proofreading Marks

Use the proofreading marks to write the sentences correctly.

> ≡   - Change a small letter to a capital letter.
> /   - Change a capital letter to a small letter.
> ∧   - Add letters, words, sentences, or punctuation marks.
> ℘   - Take out letters, words, sentences, or punctuation marks.

1 mary Poppins flies in with her umbrella.
    <u>≡</u>

_____

2 Mary Poppins Flies in with her umbrella.

_____

3 Have you read the magazie?
        ∧   ∧
       ever   n

_____

4 Have you has ever read the maogazine?

_____

Unit 4 Nicknames

Pre-read

a Do you have a nickname?

b Why do you have that nickname?

c Who is 'Figure Queen'?

d Who was 'Vacuum Cleaner' during World Cup 2002?

Track 04

Do you have a nickname?

What is your nickname?

How do you feel about your nickname?

Why do you have a nickname like that?

Sport stars and entertainers have nicknames.

Those nicknames appeal to their audiences;

so many people remember them easily.

Who is 'Vacuum Cleaner'?

Who is 'Figure Queen'?

Who has the 'Killing Smile'?

Who is 'Woman Rain'?

And who are 'F4'?

Word Listening

Listen and check.

1 ⓐ  ⓑ  ⓒ

2 ⓐ  ⓑ  ⓒ

Listen and write.

appeal	nickname	audiences

3 Hi, Red! My name is Anne!

What is your

☐☐☐☐☐☐☐ ?

4 Those nicknames ☐☐☐☐☐

to their ☐☐☐☐☐☐☐ -

☐ .

P·a·r·t 2 Picture Reading

Trace and read the story aloud.

Killing Smile appeal **entertainers** nickname **remember**

1 Why do you have a ⟨Chief⟩ , ⟨Shorty⟩ , ⟨Red⟩ like that?

nickname

2 Sport stars and 🖼 have nicknames.

entertainers

3 Those nicknames 🖼 to their audiences.

appeal

4 So, many people 🖼 them easily.

remember

5 Who has the ' 🖼 '?

Killing Smile

22

Reading Power II

Core Reading

1 This story is about _____.

ⓐ names   ⓑ nicknames   ⓒ F4

2 The singer is called the female version of Rain. She is very popular with the title song 'I Am Crazy' and the chair dance. Who is she?

ⓐ Rain   ⓑ Son, Dambi

ⓒ Wonder Girls

Reading Power III

Metaphors

Choose a word from the box to complete each metaphor.

• A metaphor is a comparison of two unlike people or things using 'to be.' A metaphor does not use 'like' or 'as', as in a simile.

| Figure Queen | F4 | Vacuum Cleaner | Woman Rain |

1

Namil Kim is a

_____.

2

Yuna Kim is a

_____.

3

Son, Dambi is a

_____.

4

The 4 characters are

_____.

Unit 5
Robin Hood; the Good Thief

Pre-read

ⓐ Have you read *Robin Hood*?

ⓑ What did he do? What was his job?

ⓒ Where did he live?

Track 05

In England, there was a good thief, Robin Hood.

He lived with his friends in Sherwood Forest.

Robin and his friends were thieves.

But, they were different from other thieves.

They stole money and treasures from bad, rich people

and gave them to poor people.

So, the poor people loved Robin Hood.

He was a good bowman.

Now, we have one question.

Was he real?

Many scholars have studied that.

But, the most important thing is that

we need ROBIN HOOD today!

Listening Power

Word Listening ♪ Track 05

Listen and check.

1 ⓐ    ⓑ   ⓒ

2 ⓐ    ⓑ

Listen and write.

thieves	from	stole

3  Robin and his friends were

☐☐☐☐☐☐☐ .

4  They ☐☐☐☐ money and

 treasures ☐☐☐ bad, rich

people and gave them to poor people.

P·a·r·t 2 Picture Reading

Trace and read the story aloud.

Sherwood Forest   bowman   **need**   scholars   **thief**

1 In England, there was a good , Robin Hood.

thief

2 He lived with his friends in .

Sherwood Forest

3 Robin Hood was a good .

bowman

4 Many have studied that.

scholars

5 But, the most important thing is that we ROBIN HOOD today!

need

Core Reading

1 This story is about _____.

   ⓐ Little John   ⓑ Robin Williams   ⓒ Robin Hood

2 Where did Robin Hood and his friends live?

   ⓐ In Seoul Forest.
   ⓑ In the Magic Tree House.
   ⓒ In Sherwood Forest.

Reading Power III

Reference Words

Read the story again. Then, write the word that each reference word refers to.

1 He lived with his friends in Sherwood Forest.

   ➡ He = _____ his = _____

2 But, they were different from others.

   ➡ they = _____ others = _____

3 They stole money and treasures from bad, rich people and gave them to poor people.

   ➡ them = _____

4 So, the poor people loved him.

   ➡ him = _____

Unit 6 Edelweiss

Pre-read

ⓐ What kind of movies do you like?

ⓑ Do you like musicals?

ⓒ Have you seen, *The Sound of Music*?

Track 06

"Edelweiss, edelweiss.

Every morning you greet me.

Small and white, clean and bright,

you look happy to meet me.

Blossom of snow, may you bloom and grow.

Bloom and grow forever.

Edelweiss, edelweiss.

Bless my homeland forever."

Do you know this song?

This song was sung by Julie Andrews in, *The Sound of Music*.

This movie is known as a classic musical,

and many of its songs are loved by people all over the world.

Are you ready? Now, let's sing together.

Listening Power
Word Listening
Track 06

Listen and check.

1   ⓐ    ⓑ    ⓒ

2   ⓐ    ⓑ

Listen and write.

Blossom of snow   musical

3   [ ][ ][ ][ ][ ][ ][ ][ ]
[ ][ ][ ] , may you bloom and grow.

4   This movie is known as a classic
[ ][ ][ ][ ][ ][ ][ ] .

1965

P·a·r·t 2 Picture Reading

Trace and read the story aloud.

| **Bless** | bloom | **bright** | sing | **songs** |

1 Small and white, clean and ⬡ , you look happy to meet me.

bright

2 Blossom of snow, may you ⬡ and grow. Bloom and grow forever.

bloom

3 Edelweiss, edelweiss. ⬡ my homeland forever.

Bless

4 Many of its ⬡ are loved by people all over the world.

songs

5 Are you ready? Now, let's ⬡ together.

sing

30

P·a·r·t 3

Reading Power II

Core Reading

1 This story is about _____.

   a the flower "Edelweiss"   **b** the song "Edelweiss"

   c many songs

2 What song can you hear in the movie, *The Sound of Music*?

   a A Spoonful of Sugar

   b Edelweiss

   c Feed the Birds

 P·a·r·t 4

Reading Power III

Homophones

Write the correct homophone for each picture.

to two too	no know	by buy bye	meat meet

1   *to Suzy*   :   **2**

       _____ : _____

2   :

       _____ : _____

3   *Sung by Julie Andrews*   :   *LEMONADE*

       _____ : _____

4   *7+3=☐*   *I know!*   :

       _____ : _____

Unit 7

Birds Never Lose Their Home!

Pre-read

ⓐ What is instinct?

ⓑ What are your instincts?

ⓒ What are some animals' instincts that you know?

Track 07

Animals have instincts.

Of course, human beings have them, too.

When babies feel hungry, they need some food.

When we are sick, we immediately look for our mothers.

When we are tired, we want to sleep.

Birds never lose their way home.

We call it, "a homing instinct".

When birds fly south in the winter,

how do they know where to go?

How do they know how to get there?

When birds return in spring,

how can they get back to the same place they left?

Trout and salmon have a homing instinct, too.

32

Listen and check.

1

2   ⓐ   ⓑ

Listen and write.

Trout and salmon	**instincts**

3      Animals have

☐☐☐☐☐☐☐☐☐ .

4

☐☐☐☐☐ ☐☐☐

☐☐☐☐☐ have a

homing instinct, too.

P·a·r·t 2 Picture Reading

Trace and read the story aloud.

| fly south | return | human beings | lose | a homing instinct |

1 Of course, have them, too.

human beings

2 Birds never their way home.

lose

3 We call it, " ".

a homing instinct

4 When birds in the winter, how do they know where to go?

fly south

5 When birds in spring, how can they get back to the same place they left?

return

34

Part 3 Core Reading

1 **This story is about** _____ .

    ⓐ trout and salmon   ⓑ homesickness
    ⓒ birds' homing instincts

2 **Which of the following about the reading is NOT true?**

    ⓐ Animals have instincts.
    ⓑ We, human beings, have instincts.
    ⓒ Trout and salmon don't have homing instincts.

Reading Power III

Part 4 The Birds' Compass

Scientists don't know exactly how the homing ability works.
Some scientists believe that …

ⓐ Birds use the positions of the sun and stars.
ⓑ Birds use the earth's magnetic field.
ⓒ Birds follow roads.
ⓓ Birds use memories of smells near their home.
ⓔ Birds use memories of familiar coastlines, river valleys, and mountain ridges.

Unit 8
Giraffes; the Beanpole

Pre-read

ⓐ Have you seen giraffes? Where did you first see them?

ⓑ Have you heard giraffes' crying? Was it mute?

ⓒ Where do giraffes live?

Track 08

Do you like giraffes?

They are tall and elegant.

Many kids want to see them.

They are not just big but are big and tall.

Especially, they have long necks and legs.

Giraffes can move very fast

and jump over fences and streams gracefully.

When giraffes gallop, all four feet are often off the ground.

Giraffes are stronger than lions.

They can kick and kill lions with their back legs.

But, don't be afraid of them.

They have long eyelashes, and they look gentle.

Many people think giraffes are cute animals.

Do you agree?

Part 1 Word Listening

Track 08

Listen and check.

1 ⓐ  ⓑ  ⓒ

2 ⓐ  ⓑ

Listen and write.

jump over fences	kick

3  Giraffes can move very fast and

☐☐☐☐ ☐☐☐☐

☐☐☐☐☐☐ and streams

gracefully.

4 They can ☐☐☐☐ and kill lions

with their back legs.

P·a·r·t 2 Picture Reading

Trace and read the story aloud.

agree	eyelashes	giraffes	kids	streams

1 Do you like ? They are tall and elegant.

giraffes

2 Many want to see them.

kids

3 Giraffes can move very fast and jump over fences and

gracefully.

streams

4 They have long , and they look gentle.

eyelashes

5 Do you ?

agree

Reading Power II

Core Reading

1 This story is about _____.

  ⓐ giraffes   ⓑ lions   ⓒ kids

2 The giraffe's nickname is 'Beanpole.' Why do they have a nickname like that?

  ⓐ Giraffes can move very fast.
  ⓑ Giraffes are stronger than lions.
  ⓒ Giraffes are the tallest of all
     land animals.

Part 4

Reading Power III

Problem Solving

1 There were 7 giraffes lowering their heads to drink. A lion scared 3 of them away. How many giraffes were left?

  ➡ _____ giraffes

2 There were 9 giraffes. 5 more came. Then, how many were there?

  ➡ _____ giraffes

Unit 9 First-Aid Kits

Pre-read

ⓐ What do you do when you get a scratch on your knee?

ⓑ Do you have a first-aid kit at home?

ⓒ What are things in it?

Track 09

We prepare first-aid kits at home.

When we sharpen a pencil,

we may cut our fingers.

When we fall down,

we may get a scratch on our knee.

It always happens suddenly,

so we need a first-aid kit.

What are things in it?

There are bandages, alcohol, painkillers,

plasters, patches, cottons, aspirins, and so on.

When we go camping or traveling, we need one.

We may face accidents suddenly,

so we must get ready for poisons, sickness, insects, and injuries.

Word Listening · Track 09

Listen and check.

1   ⓐ   ⓑ   ⓒ

2   ⓐ    ⓑ

Listen and write.

go camping	first-aid kits

3      We prepare

□□□□□□□□

□□□□ at home.

4   When we □□

□□□□□□□ or

traveling, we need one.

Part 2 Picture Reading

Trace and read the story aloud.

bandages   cut   first-aid kit   injuries   a scratch

1 When we sharpen a pencil, we may [image] our fingers.

cut

2 When we fall down, we may get [image] on our knee.

a scratch

3 It always happens suddenly, so we need a [image] .

first-aid kit

4 There are [image] , alcohol, painkillers, plasters, patches, cottons, aspirins, and so on.

bandages

5 We may face accidents suddenly, so we must get ready for poisons, sickness, insects, and [image] .

injuries

P·a·r·t
3

Reading Power II

Core Reading

1 This story is about _____.

    ⓐ body kits   ⓑ drum kits   ⓒ first-aid kits

2 What CAN'T you find in a first-aid kit?

    ⓐ bandages   ⓑ baskets
    ⓒ painkillers

P·a·r·t
4

Reading Power III

Picture Clues

Write the square name. Start at 0 and go over/up.

1 band-aids   (over _____ , up _____)

2 tweezers   (over _____ , up _____)

3 ointment   (over _____ , up _____)

4 first-aid guide   (over _____ , up _____)

Unit 10
World Countries I — England

Pre-read

(a) What is the capital of England?

(b) Who is the famous writer from England?

(c) Do you know any of Shakespeare's plays?

Track 10

England is in Europe.

England is called 'Britain' or 'The United Kingdom.'

London is the capital of England.

They speak English and use the Euro as their money.

Many people work in service industries.

London is one of the largest seaports in Europe.

We can see many historic sites

and persons in London.

They are Westminster Abbey, Big Ben,

Oxford Dictionary, Beatles, Laurence Olivier,

Shakespeare, and so on.

People from all over the world want to visit London.

Many people still love Shakespeare's plays,

Beatles' songs, and Olivier's movies.

Listening Power

Word Listening

Track 10

Listen and check.

1 (a)    (b)    (c)

2 (a)   (b)   (c)

Listen and write.

Euro	capital

3    London is the

☐☐☐☐☐☐ of England.

4    They speak English and use the

☐☐☐☐ as their money.

P·a·r·t 2 Picture Reading

Trace and read the story aloud.

Westminster Abbey	**historic**	**plays**
The United Kingdom	**seaports**	

1 England is called 'Britain' or ' .'

The United Kingdom

2 London is one of the largest in Europe.

seaports

3 We can see many sites and persons in London.

historic

4 They are , Big Ben, Oxford Dictionary, Beatles, Laurence Olivier, Shakespeare, and so on.

Westminster Abbey

5 Many people still love Shakespeare's , Beatles' songs, and Olivier's movies.

plays

P·a·r·t 3 Core Reading

1 This story is about _____

   a England
   b The U.K.(The United Kingdom)
   c Europe

2 The United Kingdom is a small country. What is the capital city of the U.K.?

   a Britain
   b Big Ben
   c London

P·a·r·t 4 Reading for Details

   a Laurence Olivier, Baron Olivier, was an English actor, director, and producer. (1907-1989)

   b William Shakespeare wrote tragedies, such as, "Hamlet", "King Lear", and "Macbeth". He is the greatest writer in the English language.(1564-1616)

   c The Beatles were a rock and pop band from England. They sang, "Let It Be", "Hey Jude", "Yesterday", "Yellow Submarine", etc.

   d Big Ben is the nickname for the great clock tower in London.

Unit 11
World Countries II
– Spain

Pre-read

ⓐ What is the capital of Spain?

ⓑ What is the famous dance in Spain?

ⓒ Who is the famous painter from Spain?

Track 11

Spain is in Europe.

Madrid is the capital of Spain.

Spain is called 'España'.

Spanish people have passion and

enjoy flamenco dancing and parties.

'Fiesta' means party.

Spanish people gather at plazas and

drink, talk, and dance all night.

Then, they eat chocolate bars at dawn and go home.

They have a special time in the afternoon.

They call it, 'Siesta'. It means 'nap'.

Most shops are closed from 2:00 p.m. to 4:00 p.m.

Also Cervantes is a famous writer from Spain.

'Don Quixote de la Mancha' is his masterpiece.

Also, the Spanish love bullfighting.

However, now some people think it is too cruel.

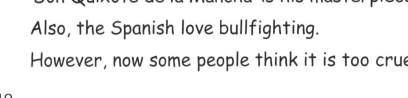

Word Listening
Track 11

Listen and check.

1 Ⓐ Ⓑ Ⓒ

2 Ⓐ Ⓑ

Listen and write.

Spain	flamenco

3 │││││ is called 'España'.

4 Spanish people have passion and enjoy

│││││││ dancing

and parties.

P·a·r·t 2 Picture Reading

Trace and read the story aloud.

Cervantes   closed   cruel   dawn   masterpiece

1 Then, they eat chocolate bars at _____ and go home.

dawn

2 Most shops are _____ from 2:00 p.m. to 4:00 p.m.

closed

3 Also _____ is a famous writer from Spain.

Cervantes

4 'Don Quixote de la Mancha' is his _____ .

masterpiece

5 Some people think bullfighting is too _____ .

cruel

50

Part 3

Core Reading

1 This story is about _____ .

    ⓐ Spain   ⓑ Flamenco   ⓒ Cervantes

2 This is a nap during the hottest part of the day. For two or three hours, shops close, and people close their eyes. What is it?

    ⓐ Fiesta   ⓑ Siesta
    ⓒ Toro

Part 4

Reading for Details

  ⓐ Don Quixote de la Mancha is a novel written by Miguel de Cervantes Saavedra.

  ⓑ Flamenco is a Spanish dance with guitar music and stepping sounds.

  ⓒ A Fiesta is a festival or religious holiday celebrated in Spanish-speaking countries.

  ⓓ Toro is a bullfight. Toro is a traditional spectacle in which people fight and kill bulls.

Unit 12 World Countries III – Australia

Pre-read

a What is the capital of Australia?

b When it is summer in Korea, what season is it in Australia?

c What is the famous building in Australia?

Track 12

Canberra is the capital of Australia.

Australians speak English.

Their ancestors emigrated from England.

Koalas are one of the famous animals in Australia.

Kangaroos, wallabies, wombats, and possums live in Australia.

Australia is the smallest continent in the world.

In Australia, Australians and Aborigines live together.

Sydney is one of the main cities in Australia.

There is an opera house in Sydney.

It looks like a sail.

Many travelers visit there.

Australia is located in the Southern hemispere,

so Australians enjoy Christmas in summer.

Have you seen the movie, *Finding Nemo*?

You can see the city, Sydney, and the opera house in that movie.

Word Listening

Track 12

Listen and check.

1 **a**  **b**  **c**

2 **a**   **b**

Listen and write.

Aborigines	wallabies	wombats

3

Kangaroos,

☐☐☐☐☐☐☐☐ ,

☐☐☐☐☐☐ , and possums

live in Australia.

4

In Australia, Australians and

☐☐☐☐☐☐☐☐☐

live together.

P·a·r·t 2 Picture Reading

Trace and read the story aloud.

| **Sydney** | ancestors | **capital** | continent | **sail** |

1 Canberra is the of Australia.

capital

2 Their emigrated from England.

ancestors

3 Australia is the smallest in the world.

continent

4 There is an opera house in .

Sydney

5 It looks like a . Many travelers visit there.

sail

Part 3
Core Reading

1 This story is about _____.

    a Canberra   b Austria   c Australia

2 Which animals live in Australia?

    a Koalas, kangaroos, platypuses, and zebras live in Australia.
    b Koalas, kangaroos, wallabies, and wombats live in Australia.
    c Kangaroos, wombats, emus, and tigers live in Australia.

Part 4

Reading Power III

Reading for Details

Marsupial mothers carry their babies in a pouch on their lower belly.

    a A kangaroo is an Australian marsupial. It moves by jumping on its back legs.
    b A koala is an Australian marsupial. It has grey fur and lives in gum trees.
    c A wombat is an Australian marsupial. It looks like a small bear.
    d A wallaby looks like a small kangaroo. Wallabies live in Australia and New Zealand.

Unit 13
World Countries IV – America

Pre-read

a What is the capital of the USA?

b Who is the president of the USA?

c What are famous universities in the USA?

Track 13

Washington, D.C. is the capital of the United States.

The United States has another name, America.

There are 48 states in America.

There are many famous places in America.

They are the Grand Canyon, Niagara Falls, Disneyland,

Hollywood, Broadway, Wall Street, and so on.

Many people want to visit New York,

and people in New York are called 'New Yorkers.'

Mark Twain, Edgar Allen Poe,

and Ernest Miller Hemingway were born in America.

They left us many masterpieces.

James Dean, Marilyn Monroe, Vivian Leigh,

and Clark Gable are legendary movie stars.

Furthermore, America is the center of world trade and the economy.

America is the leader of the world now.

Word Listening
Track 13

Listen and check.

1 ⓐ    ⓑ

2 ⓐ   ⓑ   ⓒ

Listen and write.

legendary	world trade	economy

3  James Dean, Marilyn Monroe, Vivian Leigh, and Clark Gable are

☐☐☐☐☐☐☐☐☐

movie stars.

4  America is the center of

☐☐☐☐☐☐☐☐☐

and the ☐☐☐☐☐☐☐ .

P·a·r·t 2
Picture Reading

Trace and read the story aloud.

| Grand Canyon | leader | masterpieces |
| New Yorkers | America | |

1 There are many famous places in [image] .

America

2 They are the [image] , Niagara Falls, Disneyland, Hollywood, Broadway, Wall Street, and so on.

Grand Canyon

3 Many people want to visit New York, and people in New York are called ' [image] .'

New Yorkers

4 Mark Twain, Edgar Allen Poe, and Ernest Miller Hemingway were born in America. They left us many [image] .

masterpieces

5 America is the [image] of the world now.

leader

58

P·a·r·t 3 Core Reading

1 This story is about _____.

ⓐ North America　　ⓑ the United States　　ⓒ New York

2 What place can you visit when you go sightseeing in America?

ⓐ the Grand Canyon
ⓑ Clark Gable
ⓒ Edgar Allen Poe

P·a·r·t 4

Reading Power III

Reading for Details

ⓐ Marilyn Monroe was an American actress, singer, and model. (1926-1962)

ⓑ Mark Twain was an American author.(1835-1910) He wrote "The Adventures of Huckleberry Finn" and "The Adventures of Tom Sawyer."

ⓒ Disneyland is an American amusement park.

ⓓ Wall Street is a narrow street in New York where the New York and the American Stock Exchanges, as well as many banks, are located.

Disneyland

Mark Twain

Marilyn Monroe

Wall Street

Unit 14 Essay about Me

Pre-read

ⓐ Think about yourself. How old are you?
Where were you born?

ⓑ Are you kind? Are you tall? Are you cute?

ⓒ How about your family members?
Are they kind, tall, and cute?

Track 14

Think about yourself. How was your life so far?

Where were you born?

How old are you? What grade are you in?

Do you have a boyfriend or girlfriend?

Who is your best friend?

What's your hobby? Do you play sports?

What do you do on Sundays or holidays?

Do you like pink or blue? What color do you like?

What is your favorite subject?

Do you like watching movies?

Let's talk about your friends.

Ask your friends some questions.

Then, make a chart.

Part 1 Word Listening

Track 14

Listen and check.

1 ⓐ    ⓑ

2 ⓐ 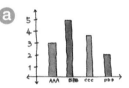   ⓑ 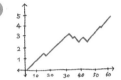   ⓒ

Listen and write.

What grade	yourself	in

3  You!

Think about

☐☐☐☐☐☐☐ .

How was your life so far?

4  I'm 12. I'm a 5th grader.

How old are you? ☐☐☐☐

☐☐☐☐☐ are you ☐☐ ?

P·a·r·t 2 Picture Reading

Trace and read the story aloud.

born   grade   holidays   life   subject

1 Think about yourself. How was your ⊢—→ YEARS so far?

life

2 Where were you ?

born

3 How old are you? What are you in?

grade

4 What do you do on Sundays or ?

holidays

5 What is your favorite ?

subject

P·a·r·t 3 Core Reading

1 This story is about _____.

    a my friends   **b** my hobbies   **c** myself

2 How old are you? What grade are you in?

    I am _____ years old.

    I am in the _____ grade.

P·a·r·t 4 Me Webs

Complete the webs.

> **a** What is your name? How old are you?
> **b** How many family members do you have?
> **c** Where do you like to go?
> **d** What is your hobby?
> **e** What is your favorite food?
> **f** Do you play with your friends? Who is your best friend?

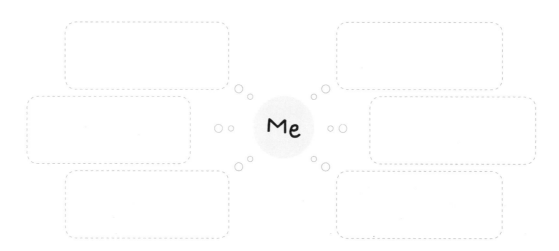

Unit 15

The Origin of Songs

Pre-read

ⓐ Do you like singing?

ⓑ What is your favorite song?

ⓒ What kind of music do you like?

Popular songs, classical music, or opera?

Track 15

When did human beings first start singing?

Historians think it was connected with religion.

People's songs showed their respect for God.

Singing is still important in a lot of religions.

Buddhists and Christians sing for their God.

And, the ancients sang when they worked.

Slaves sang when they felt sad;

soldiers sang when they marched;

farmers sang when they planted and harvested crops;

and fishermen sang when they fished.

Songs have always been a part of human beings' lives.

When do you sing?

Listening Power

Word Listening

Track 15

Listen and check.

1 ⓐ  ⓑ   ⓒ

2 ⓐ   ⓑ  ⓒ

Listen and write.

sing for their God	respect

3 People's songs showed their

⬜⬜⬜⬜⬜⬜ for God.

4 Buddhists and Christians ⬜⬜⬜⬜

⬜⬜⬜ ⬜⬜⬜⬜⬜

⬜⬜⬜.

P·a·r·t 2 Picture Reading

Trace and read the story aloud.

| Songs | sing | connected | worked | marched |

1 Historians think it was [songs ←→ religion] with religion.

connected

2 And, the ancients sang when they [image] .

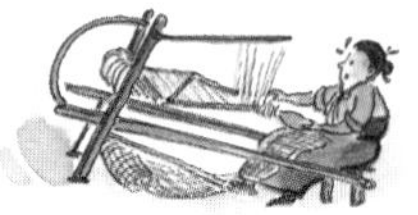

worked

3 Slaves sang when they felt sad; soldiers sang when they [image] ; and farmers sang when they planted and harvested crops.

marched

4 [image] [image] have always been a part of human beings' lives.

Songs

5 When do you [image] ?

sing

Core Reading

1 This story is about _____.

   a religions   **b** human beings
   c the origin of songs

2 Which of the following about the reading is NOT true?

   a Historians don't think singing was connected with religion.
   b Singing is still important in a lot of religions.
   c Songs have always been a part of human beings' lives.

P·a·r·t 4

Writing Power

Making Sentences

Use the words in the box to complete the sentences.

1   Historians think   •   •   been a part of human beings' lives.

2   Singing is still important   •   •   for their God.

3   Buddhists and Christians sing   •   •   in a lot of religions.

4   Songs have always   •   •   it was connected with religion.

Unit 16 Living Together

Pre-read

ⓐ What are homeless people?

ⓑ Where do you see them?

ⓒ How do we help them?

Track 16

We can see people sleeping in underpasses at night.

They look very poor and hungry.

Why do they choose that life?

These days, we have economical difficulties.

So, many people lose their jobs and also lose hope.

Some children cannot afford lunch.

Some old people are sick,

but no one takes care of them.

How do we help them? What can we do for them?

Many volunteers provide meals to them.

Some take care of orphans.

Some make a donation to them in secret.

Various people live in our community together,

and we have to help each other.

Word Listening

Listen and check.

1

2

Listen and write.

economical	lose their jobs

3  These days, we have

☐☐☐☐☐☐☐☐☐

difficulties.

4  Many people ☐☐☐☐

 ☐☐☐☐☐☐☐ and

also lose hope.

P·a·r·t 2 Picture Reading

Trace and read the story aloud.

community   donation   lunch   orphans   underpasses

1 We can see people sleeping in at night.

underpasses

2 Some children cannot afford .

lunch

3 Some take care of .

orphans

4 Some make a to them in secret.

donation

5 Various people live in our together, and we have to help each other.

community

70

P·a·r·t

3

Reading Power II

Core Reading

1 This story is about _____.

    ⓐ living alone   ⓑ living together
    ⓒ living in the wild

2 Which of the following about the reading is true?

    ⓐ We can't see people sleeping in underpasses at night.
    ⓑ Some people take care of homeless animals.
    ⓒ Some people take care of orphans.

P·a·r·t

4

Reading Power III

Problem Solving

Write the answers.

1 Peter put 48 apples in baskets. He put 6 apples in each basket. How many baskets did he fill?

    ➡ _____ baskets

2 Suzy donated 56 loaves of bread in 7 days. She donated the same number of loaves each day. How many loaves of bread did she donate each day?

    ➡ _____ loaves of bread

Unit 17 Mother Love

Pre-read

ⓐ Who is 'MOM' for you?

ⓑ When do you feel your mom's love?

ⓒ Do animals have 'mother love'? What do you think?

Track 17

What is the greatest love in the world?

Maybe it's 'MOTHER LOVE.'

All mothers love their babies.

That is very special and absolute.

Who is Mom for you?

Mother always wakes me up in the morning.

She keeps nagging me all the time,

"Study hard. Be nice."

Is it right?

But, we overlook something important.

That's MOTHER LOVE behind her nagging.

Open your mind's eyes big and look at your mom again.

Then, you can see her great love for us.

Word Listening

Track 17

Listen and check.

1 ⓐ  ⓑ  ⓒ

2 ⓐ  ⓑ  ⓒ

Listen and write.

love their babies	nagging

3  All mothers ☐☐☐☐ ☐☐☐☐ ☐☐☐☐☐ .

4  She keeps ☐☐☐☐☐☐☐ me all the time, "Study hard. Be nice."

P·a·r·t 2 Picture Reading

Trace and read the story aloud.

MOTHER LOVE   absolute   **mind's eyes**
greatest love   **overlook**

1 What is the ♥♥♥ in the world?

greatest love

2 That is very special and .

absolute

3 Is it right? But, we something important.

overlook

4 That's behind her nagging.

MOTHER LOVE

5 Open your big and look at your mom again.

mind's eyes

74

3 Core Reading

1 This story is about _____.

ⓐ parental respect   ⓑ a father's love
ⓒ a mother's love

2 The woman brings you up. She keeps nagging you all the time, "Study hard. Be nice." She loves you forever. Who is she?

ⓐ grandfather
ⓑ father
ⓒ mother

Reading Power III

4 Sequencing

Number the pictures to show the order of the story.

1

2

3

4

Unit 18 — Picture Writing

Pre-read

ⓐ How did the ancients write their thoughts before letters?

ⓑ Where do we see picture writings?

ⓒ Can you write a letter to your friend using picture writings?

Track 18

How did the ancients communicate to each other before letters?

How do historians find out about ancient people's lives?

Ancient people rode a horse, ate meat, used fires, and so on.

We know these facts from wall paintings.

There are many wall paintings around the world.

They tell us a lot of things about ancient people's lives.

There are pictures of wars, dances, festivals,

vehicles, foods, clothes, religions, weapons,

hunting methods, and so on.

Some pictures were found in caves.

Some pictures were found in kings' tombs.

Many people lived before letters were invented.

They loved, fought, and studied all their life.

Therefore, we can now live conveniently, and our culture can develop.

Listening Power

Word Listening Track 18

Listen and check.

1 ⓐ   ⓑ  ⓒ

2 ⓐ  ⓑ  ⓒ

Listen and write.

find out	culture can develop

3    How do historians ☐ ☐ ☐ ☐

☐ ☐ ☐ about ancient people's lives?

4

We can now live conveniently, and our

☐ ☐ ☐ ☐ ☐ ☐ ☐ ☐ ☐

☐ ☐ ☐ ☐ ☐ ☐ .

P·a·r·t
2 Picture Reading

Trace and read the story aloud.

fires   **letters**   **tombs**   **weapons**   **wall paintings**

1   Ancient people rode a horse, ate meat, used , and so on.

fires

2   There are many around the world.

wall paintings

3   There are pictures of wars, dances, festivals, vehicles, foods, clothes, religions, , hunting methods, and so on.

weapons

4   Some pictures were found in kings' .

tombs

5   Many people lived before were invented.

letters

78

P·a·r·t 3 Core Reading

1 This story is about _____ .

ⓐ letters   ⓑ wall paintings   ⓒ sign language

2 Which of the following about the reading is NOT true?

ⓐ We can know our city life in the wall paintings.
ⓑ There are many wall paintings around the world.
ⓒ Some pictures were found in caves.

P·a·r·t 4 Picture Clues - Cave Drawings

1  •   •

2  •   • 

3  •   • 

Unit 19 Fun Cartoon Characters

Pre-read

ⓐ What's your favorite cartoon?

ⓑ Who are the main characters?

ⓒ Why do you like that cartoon and those characters?
Can you draw them?

Track 19

How do you spend your free time?

Most children grab the remote control

and watch TV programs.

Children like cartoons very much

because they can see fun characters on them.

Some characters can do magic and fly in the sky.

Some have a magic pocket and can get anything they want.

There are good monsters and talking donkeys in cartoons.

A brave prince saves a princess, and they get married.

Of course, there are bad characters,

such as Captain Hook, Cinderella's step mother, and sisters, and so on.

Cartoons can have good or bad effects on children.

So, their parents must guide them and tell them what is right and

wrong.

P·a·r·t 1 Word Listening

Track 19

Listen and check.

1 **a**  **b** **c**

2 **a** **b**

Listen and write.

cartoons	do magic

3  Children like ⬚⬚⬚⬚⬚⬚⬚-

⬚ very much because they can see fun

characters on them.

4  Some characters can ⬚⬚

⬚⬚⬚⬚ and fly in the sky.

P·a·r·t 2 Picture Reading

Trace and read the story aloud.

| bad effects | free time | donkeys |
| magic pocket | step mother | |

1 How do you spend your   ?

free time

2 Some have a   and can get anything they want.

magic pocket

3 There are good monsters and talking   in cartoons.

donkeys

4 Of course, there are bad characters, such as Captain Hook,

Cinderella's   and sisters, and so on.

step mother

5 Cartoons can have good or   on children.

bad effects

Part 3 Core Reading

1 This story is about _____.

ⓐ Captain Hook   ⓑ Cinderella
ⓒ cartoon characters

2 The character is from the picture book written and illustrated by William Steig. He is a large, green monster (ogre+human). He lives in a swamp. Who is he?

ⓐ Princess Fiona   ⓑ Shrek   ⓒ Donkey

Part 4 Reading for Details

ⓐ Doraemon is a robotic cat. He can take out devices from his fourth-dimensional pocket. He travels back in time from the 22nd century to help a schoolboy.

ⓑ Dooly is a baby dinosaur. He uses super powers in times of danger. He points his right finger and shouts "Hoihoi!"

ⓒ Nemo is a young clownfish. Marlin is his father. One of Nemo's fins is smaller than the other. Marlin calls Nemo's smaller fin "Lucky Fin."

ⓓ SpongeBob SquarePants works as a cook in 'Bikini Bottom,' under the sea. He wears a white shirt with a red tie and brown square pants.

Unit 20 Fruit Bat–the Flying Fox

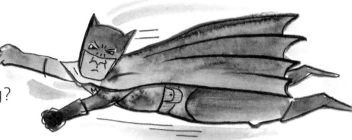

Pre-read

ⓐ Have you ever seen a bat?

ⓑ Have you ever seen a fox flying?

ⓒ Why does it have that name?

Track 20

Have you ever heard or seen a flying fox?

Aha! Batman can fly. But he is not real.

A flying fox is real.

What is it? It's a bat.

Why does it have that name?

A flying fox's face looks like a fox's face.

And, its size is bigger than others.

Foxes eat meat. But, flying foxes eat fruit.

That's why we call them, 'Fruit Bats.'

Does everybody like them? Do you like bats?

Most people do not like bats.

Bats hang upside down on branches or in caves.

Their features look ugly.

However, all bats are not harmful.

84

Word Listening

Track 20

Listen and check.

1

a

b

c

2

a

b

c

Listen and write.

flying foxes	hang upside down

3

Foxes eat meat.

But, ☐ ☐ ☐ ☐ ☐ ☐

☐ ☐ ☐ ☐ ☐ eat fruit.

4

Bats ☐ ☐ ☐ ☐

☐ ☐ ☐ ☐ ☐ ☐ ☐ ☐ ☐

on branches or in caves.

P·a·r·t 2 Picture Reading

Trace and read the story aloud.

Fruit Bats   bigger   **caves**   harmful   **fox's face**

1 A flying fox's face looks like a .

fox's face

2 And, its size is > than others.

bigger

3 That's why we call them, ' .'

Fruit Bats

4 Bats hang upside down on branches or in .

caves

5 Their features look ugly. However, all bats are not .

harmful

86

P·a·r·t 3

Core Reading

1 This story is about _____ .

   ⓐ fruit foxes(=flying bats)   ⓑ fruit bats(=flying foxes)
   ⓒ Batman

2 Why do they call flying foxes, 'fruit bats'?

   ⓐ Because they eat meat.
   ⓑ Because they eat fruit.
   ⓒ Because they eat insects.

P·a·r·t 4

Making Sentences

1 Have you ever heard •   • than others.

2 A flying fox's face looks •   • like bats.

3 And, its size is bigger •   • or seen a flying fox?

4 Most people do not •   • like a fox's face.

Script & Answers

Answers

Unit 1

Part 1

Listen and check.

1: It has a human's face and a monster's body.

2: If they did not, the sphinx swallowed them.

Listen and write.

3: Nobody could answer the riddle, except brave Oedipus.

4: What creature goes on four feet in the morning, two feet at noon and three in the evening?

1 ⓑ   2 ⓐ
3 Oedipus   4 creature

Part 3

1 ⓒ   2 ⓒ

Part 4

Make-Believe

Real

Make-Believe

Make-Believe

Real

Real

Unit 2

Part 1

Listen and check.

1: His full name is Ludwig van Beethoven.

2: When he was 30, he was almost deaf.

Listen and write.

3: When he was four years old, he played the harpsichord and violin.

4: He composed music and played the organ when he was only eight.

1 ⓒ   2 ⓑ
3 played the harpsichord
4 composed music

Part 3

1 ⓒ   2 ⓑ

Part 4

1 inform   2 entertain   3 persuade

Unit 3

Part 1

Listen and check.

1: Writers look over sentences and check spelling.

2: Writers proofread every detail.

Listen and write.

3: What is proofreading?

4: They also don't forget to check grammar, punctuation, and other errors.

1 ⓑ   2 ⓐ
3 proofreading   4 errors

Part 3

1 ⓒ   2 ⓑ

Part 4

1 mary Poppins flies in with her umbrella.
⇒ Mary Poppins flies in with her umbrella.

2 Mary Poppins Flies in with her umbrella.
⇒ Mary Poppins flies in with her umbrella.

3 Have you read the magazie?
⇒ Have you ever read the magazine?

4 Have you has ever read the maogazine?
⇒ Have you ever read the magazine?

90

Unit 4

Part1

Listen and check.
1: Who is 'Vacuum Cleaner'?
2: Who is 'Figure Queen'?

Listen and write.
3: What is your nickname?
4: Those nicknames appeal to their audiences.

1 ⓑ   2 ⓒ
3 nickname   4 appeal / audiences

Part3

1 ⓑ   2 ⓑ

Part4

1
Namil Kim is a
Vacuum Cleaner .

2
Yuna Kim is a
Figure Queen .

3
Son, dambi is a
Woman Rain .

4
The 4 characters are
F4 .

Unit 5

Part1

Listen and check.
1: In England, there was a good thief, Robin Hood.
2: Robin Hood was a good bowman.

Listen and write.
3: Robin and his friends were thieves.
4: They stole money and treasures from bad, rich people and gave them to poor people.

1 ⓐ   2 ⓑ
3 thieves   4 stole / from

Part3

1 ⓒ   2 ⓒ

Part4

1 He = Robin Hood   his = Robin Hood's

2 they = Robin Hood and his friends
  his = other thieves

3 them = money and treasures

4 him = Robin Hood

Unit 6

Part1

Listen and check.
1: Edelweiss, edelweiss. Every morning you greet me.
2: This song was sung by Julie Andrews in, *The Sound of Music*.

Listen and write.
3: Blossom of snow, may you bloom and grow.
4: This movie is known as a classic musical.

1 ⓒ   2 ⓑ
3 Blossom of snow
4 musical

Part3

1 ⓑ   2 ⓑ

Part4

1 :   2 :
to : two   meet : meat

3 :   4 :
by : buy   know : no

Answers

Unit 7

Part1

Listen and check.
1: When we are tired, we want to sleep.
2: Birds never lose their way home.

Listen and write.
3: Animals have instincts.
4: Trout and salmon have a homing instinct, too.

1 ⓑ   2 ⓑ
3 instincts   4 Trout and salmon

Part3

1 ⓒ   2 ⓒ

Part4

Unit 8

Part1

Listen and check.
1: When giraffes gallop, all four feet are often off the ground.
2: Giraffes are stronger than lions.

Listen and write.
3: Giraffes can move very fast and jump over fences and streams gracefully.
4: They can kick and kill lions with their back legs.

1 ⓐ   2 ⓐ
3 jump over fences
4 kick

Part3

1 ⓐ   2 ⓒ

Part4

1 4(four) giraffes
2 14(fourteen) giraffes

Unit 9

Part1

Listen and check.
1: When we sharpen a pencil, we may cut our fingers.
2: There are bandages, alcohol, painkillers, plasters, patches, cottons, aspirins, and so on.

Listen and write.
3: We prepare first-aid kits at home.
4: When we go camping or traveling, we need one.

1 ⓒ   2 ⓐ
3 first-aid kits   4 go camping

Part3

1 ⓒ   2 ⓑ

Part4

1 band-aids   (over 4 , up 1)
2 tweezers   (over 2 , up 3)
3 ointment   (over 1 , up 3)
4 first-aid guide   (over 4 , up 4)

Unit 10

Part1

Listen and check.
1: England is in Europe.
2: People from all over the world want to visit London.

Listen and write.
3: London is the capital of England.
4: They speak English and use the Euro as their money.

1 ⓑ   2 ⓒ
3 capital   4 Euro

Part3

1 ⓐ   2 ⓒ

Part4

Unit 11

Part1

Listen and check.
1: Madrid is the capital of Spain.
2: 'Fiesta' means party. Spanish people gather at plazas and drink, talk, and dance all night.

Listen and write.
3: Spain is called 'España'.
4: Spanish people have passion and enjoy flamenco dancing and parties.

1 ⓒ   2 ⓑ
3 Spain   4 flamenco

Part3

1 ⓐ   2 ⓑ

Part4

Unit 12

Part1

Listen and check.
1: Koalas are one of the famous animals in Australia.
2: Australia is located in the Southern hemisphere.

Listen and write.
3: Kangaroos, wallabies, wombats, and possums live in Australia.
4: In Australia, Australians and Aborigines live together.

1 ⓑ   2 ⓑ
3 wallabies / wombats
4 Aborigines

Part3

1 ⓒ   2 ⓑ

Part4

Unit 13

Part1

Listen and check.
1: Washington, D.C. is the capital of the United States.
2: The United States has another name, America.

Listen and write.
3: James Dean, Marilyn Monroe, Vivian Leigh, and Clark Gable are legendary movie stars.
4: America is the center of world trade and the economy.

1 ⓑ   2 ⓐ
3 legendary   4 world trade / economy

Part3

1 ⓑ   2 ⓐ

Answers

Part4

Disneyland

Mark Twain

Marilyn Monroe

Wall Street

Unit 14

Part1

Listen and check.
1: Who is your best friend?
2: Then, make a chart.

Listen and write.
3: Think about yourself. How was your life so far?
4: How old are you? What grade are you in?

1 ⓑ 　　　　2 ⓒ
3 yourself　　　4 What grade / in

Part3

1 ⓒ　　　　2 Answers may vary.

Part4

Answers may vary.

Unit 15

Part1

Listen and check.
1: Singing is still important in a lot of religions.
2: Fishermen sang when they fished.

Listen and write.
3: People's songs showed their respect for God.
4: Buddhists and Christians sing for their God.

1 ⓒ　　　　2 ⓒ
3 respect　　　4 sing for their God

Part3

1 ⓒ　　　　2 ⓐ

Part4

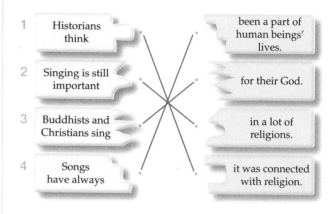

1　Historians think　·　　　·　been a part of human beings' lives.

2　Singing is still important　·　　　·　for their God.

3　Buddhists and Christians sing　·　　　·　in a lot of religions.

4　Songs have always　·　　　·　it was connected with religion.

Unit 16

Part1

Listen and check.
1: We can see people sleeping in underpasses at night.
2: Many volunteers provide meals to them.

Listen and write.
3: These days, we have economical difficulties.
4: Many people lose their jobs and also lose hope.

1 ⓒ　　　　2 ⓐ
3 economical　　4 lose their jobs

Part3

1 ⓑ　　　　2 ⓒ

Part4

1 8(eight) baskets
2 8(eight) loaves of bread

Unit 17

Part1

Listen and check.

1: Maybe it's 'MOTHER LOVE.'

2: Mother always wakes me up in the morning.

Listen and write.

3: All mothers love their babies.

4: She keeps nagging me all the time, "Study hard. Be nice."

1 **a**   2 **b**

3 love their babies

4 nagging

Part3

1 **c**   2 **c**

Part4

1    2

③

②

3    4

④

①

Unit 18

Part1

Listen and check.

1: Some pictures were found in caves.

2: Some pictures were found in kings' tombs.

Listen and write.

3: How do historians find out about ancient people's lives?

4: We can now live conveniently, and our culture can develop.

1 **a**   2 **b**

3 find out   4 culture can develop

Part3

1 **b**   2 **a**

Part4

1

2

3

Unit 19

Part1

Listen and check.

1: Most children grab the remote control and watch TV programs.

2: A brave prince saves a princess, and they get married.

Listen and write.

3: Children like cartoons very much because they can see fun characters on them.

4: Some characters can do magic and fly in the sky.

1 **b**   2 **a**

3 cartoons   4 do magic

Part3

1 **c**   2 **b**

Part4

ⓒ   ⓑ   ⓓ   ⓐ

Answers

Part1

Listen and check.

1: Aha! Batman can fly. But he is not real.

2: A flying fox's face looks like a fox's face.

Listen and write.

3: Foxes eat meat. But, flying foxes eat fruit.

4: Bats hang upside down on branches or in caves.

1 ⓑ   2 ⓒ

3 flying foxes   4 hang upside down

Part3

1 ⓑ   2 ⓑ

Part4

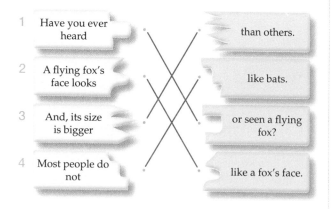

1 Have you ever heard — or seen a flying fox?

2 A flying fox's face looks — like a fox's face.

3 And, its size is bigger — than others.

4 Most people do not — like bats.

Appendixes

Self-Assessment Chart I
Complete the chart after each unit is finished.
: 하나의 unit이 끝날 때마다 스스로 체크해 보도록 합니다.

Self-Assessment Chart II
Complete the chart after each unit is finished.
: 하나의 unit이 끝날 때마다 스스로 체크해 보도록 합니다.

Self-Assessment Chart III
Complete the chart after all the units are finished.
: 모든 unit이 끝나고 스스로 체크해 보도록 합니다.

ADVICE TO TEACHERS

1. 딱딱한 수업대신 어린이들이 기분을 풀 수 있는 시간을 주세요.
2. 한 가지 파트의 수업을 오래 지속하지 마세요. 예를 들면 듣기, 읽기,
   토론하기, 쓰기 등의 각각의 파트들의 시간배당에 신경을 쓰셔야합니다.
3. 어린이들과 이야기 내용에 대해 이야기 나눠봅니다.
4. 칭찬을 많이 해 주세요.
   어린이들이 유창하게 읽는다면 크게 칭찬합니다.
   어린이들이 이야기의 내용에 대해 적절한 의견을 표한다면 칭찬합니다.
   하나의 이야기의 읽기를 모두 완성했다면 칭찬합니다.

Self-Assessment Chart I

Unit # _____ Title _____

Date _____

Name _____

		Yes	No
1	Before you read the story, were you able to predict what might happen in a story? How?	✓	
2	Listen well to the story.		
3	Do you know the meaning of all the words in the story?		
4	Repeatedly read the story aloud.		
5	Answer all the questions in the book.		
6	Tell anyone about the story.		

Self-Assessment Chart Ⅱ

Unit # _____ Title _____

Date _____

Name _____

		Yes	No
1	Observe punctuation. (구두점 활용 점검하기)	✓	
2	Read with intonation. (억양과 어조 점검하기)		
3	Read at appropriate speed. (읽기의 속도 점검하기)		
4	Read aloud to your partner. (옆 친구에게 이야기를 알아듣기 쉽게 읽어주기)		
5	Read aloud in group. (학급의 친구들 앞에서 소리 내어 바르게 읽기)		
6	Sequence the story. (이야기의 순서 및 흐름의 이해 확인하기)		
7	Talk about the theme or characters.(읽은 이야기 속의 인물들과 인물들의 성향 및 이야기의 주제를 찾아서 말하고 개인의 의견을 넣어 친구들과 의논할 수 있는지 확인하기)		
8	Relate the story to your personal experience. (읽은 이야기의 내용과 개인적인 경험들을 연관 지어 생각해보기)		

After reading all the stories in this book…

Self-Assessment Chart Ⅲ

Title _____

Name _____

		Yes	No
1	I like listening to stories.	✓	
2	I like reading stories.		
3	I like pointing at the words.		
4	I can turn pages carefully.		
5	I like re-telling stories.		
6	I know the meaning of all the words in this book.		
7	I like someone reading to me.		
8	I like guessing what is going to happen in a story.		

9 My favorite story is "_____".

The story is about _____.

10 I remember these words.

_____

_____

And, I remember these sentences.

_____

_____

_____

_____

Fun BOOK

Book 2

Iam books

The Sphinx's Riddle for Oedipus

Symphony No. 9 in D minor, op. 125, <Movement 4>

Proofreading

You're the Future!

Hi, I'm Judy. I'm from Korea.
I'm excited... The winner was recognized for his campaign to protect the environment. Look who we have here, everyone! The Big Green Help Award goes to Leonardo DiCaprio!

Thank you, Judy! Thank you, kids! We need all of you, the next generation, to be aware. You're the future!

Adventures of Robin Hood

He is good at horseback riding and shooting arrows.

He steals from the rich and gives to the poor. Guess who he is?

Ta-da! Robin Hood and his friends!

The Sound of Music

Jonathan Livingston Seagull

A Powerful Kick

Look at giraffes bending down to drink.

It's difficult and dangerous for lions to hunt giraffes.

The giraffe defends itself with a kick.

A powerful kick from a giraffe can break a lion's skull.

Do You Have First-Aid kits?

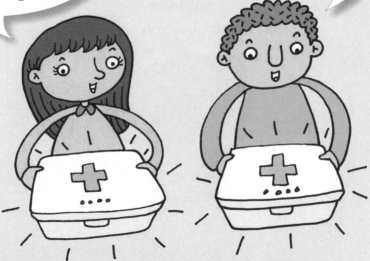

Hamlet (1948)

Siesta in Spain

Finding Nemo

1 Any of you heard of Sydney?

2 Sydney? Oh, sure!

2 Follow the E.A.C. That's the East Australian Current.

1 They know Sydney! Do you know how to get there?

1 Can't miss it. It's in that direction.

2 Thank you!

Barack Obama Took the Oath as the 44th President of the U.S.

WWW

The Origin of Songs

UNIT 16

Mindlele (Free Meals' Service)

UNIT 17

The Crow Thinks Her Own Bird Is the Fairest

When Pablo Picasso First Saw Them, He Declared in Awe

A Time of True Love's First Kiss ······

We Must Save Hodgson's Bats!